EARLY CODING CONCEPTS

GUS'S ROUTINE

A LOOPING STORY

GRASSHOPPER

by Elizabeth Everett
illustrated by Christos Skaltsas

Tools for Parents & Teachers

Grasshopper Books enhance imagination and introduce the earliest readers to fiction with fun storylines and illustrations. The easy-to-read text supports early reading experiences with repetitive sentence patterns and sight words.

Before Reading

- Look at the cover illustration. What do readers see? What do they think the book will be about?
- Look at the picture glossary together. Sound out the words. Ask readers to identify the first letter of each vocabulary word.

Read the Book

- "Walk" through the book, reading to or along with the reader. Point to the illustrations as you read.

After Reading

- Review the picture glossary again. Ask readers to locate the words in the text.
- Tell the reader: Looping is a coding instruction that tells computers to repeat the same sequence over and over again. Example: You design a sticker on the computer. You want to share it with 20 friends. You can instruct the computer to repeat the design sequence exactly 20 times.
- Ask the reader: Gus repeats a sequence every day. One day, his mom does most of the steps. It changes Gus's usual sequence. This is called branching. Can you name an example of branching in your daily routine?

Grasshopper Books are published by Jump!
5357 Penn Avenue South
Minneapolis, MN 55419
www.jumplibrary.com

Library of Congress Cataloging-in-Publication Data

Names: Everett, Elizabeth, 1978- author.
Skaltsas, Christos, illustrator.
Title: Gus's routine: a looping story / by Elizabeth Everett; illustrated by Christos Skaltsas.
Description: Minneapolis, MN: Jump!, Inc., [2023]
Series: Early coding concepts
Audience: Ages 4-7.
Identifiers: LCCN 2022030830 (print)
LCCN 2022030831 (ebook)
ISBN 9798885241762 (hardcover)
ISBN 9798885241779 (paperback)
ISBN 9798885241786 (ebook)
Subjects: LCSH: Readers (Primary)
LCGFT: Readers (Publications)
Classification: LCC PE1119.2.E944 2023 (print)
LCC PE1119.2 (ebook)
DDC 428.6/2–dc23/eng/20220715
LC record available at https://lccn.loc.gov/2022030830
LC ebook record available at https://lccn.loc.gov/2022030831

Editor: Jenna Gleisner
Direction and Layout: Anna Peterson
Illustrator: Christos Skaltsas

Printed in the United States of America at Corporate Graphics in North Mankato, Minnesota.

Table of Contents

Same Steps

Gus gets home from school.

"Hi, Max!" says Gus.

"Don't forget to walk Max!"
says Gus's mom.

Gus gets Max's leash.

Then Gus walks Max.

They walk around the block.

Max

They get home.

Gus gives Max water.

Gus feeds Max.

Max eats.

Then they play!

Gus follows this sequence each day.

Max

The next day, Gus has practice after school.

He gets home late.

Mom already walked Max.

She gave him water.

She fed him, too.

The sequence changed.

Many of the steps are already done.

Gus and Max skip right to playing!

Max

Let's Review!

Looping is a coding instruction we give computers when we want them to repeat something over and over again. Gus repeats the same tasks every day when he takes care of Max. What kinds of tasks do you think computers repeat?

Picture Glossary

changed
Became different.

sequence
A series of tasks done in a specific order.

skip
To leave something out or pass over it.

steps
Actions taken to make something happen.